First published in Great Britain by
Pendulum Gallery Press
56 Ackender Road, Alton, Hants GU34 1JS

© TONI GOFFE 1997

HOW TO MAKE WOMEN HAPPY
ISBN 0-948912-37-5

PRINTED 1997

Printed in Great Britain by
UNWIN BROTHERS LTD. OLD WOKING. SURREY

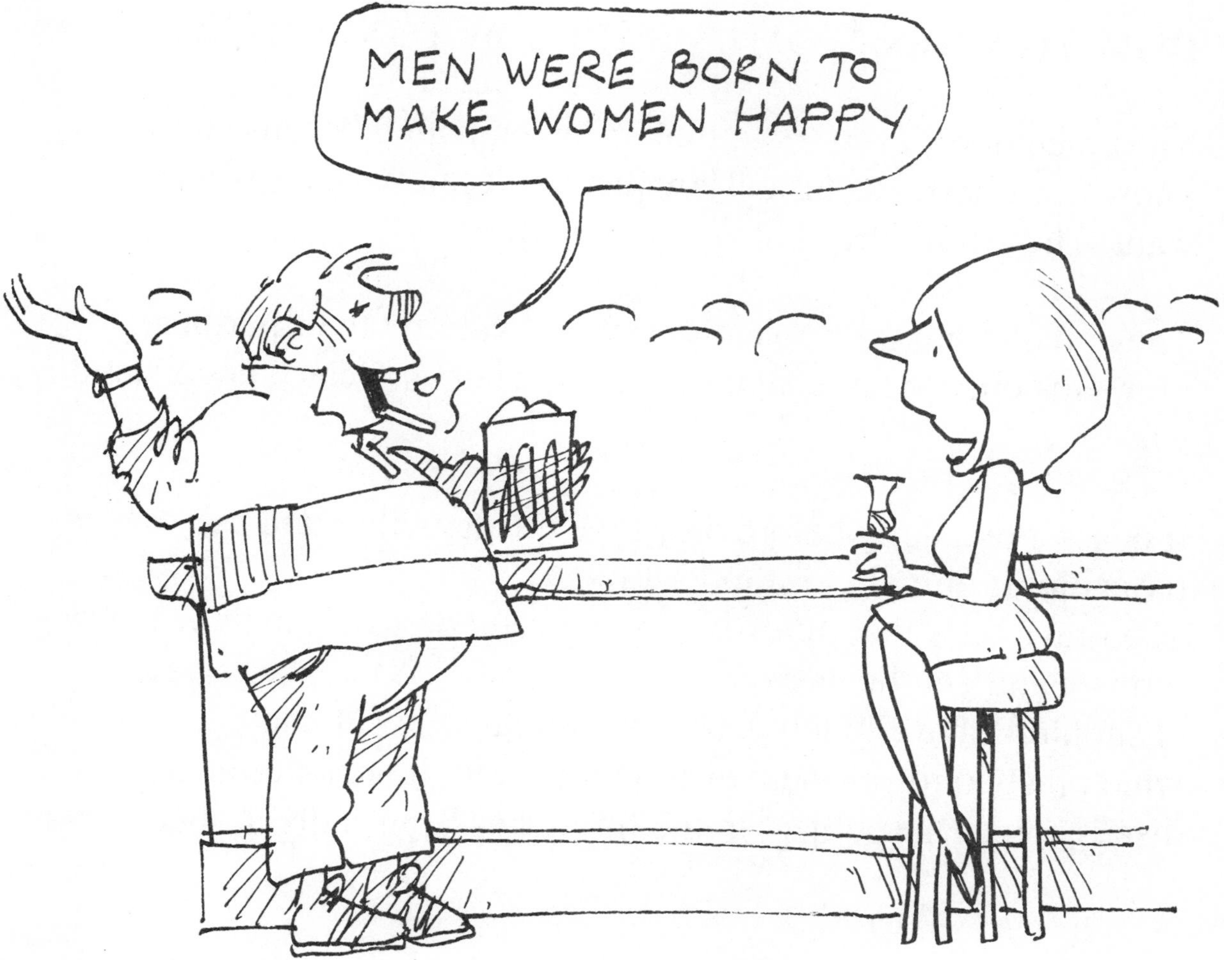
MEN WERE BORN TO MAKE WOMEN HAPPY

HOW TO MAKE WOMEN HAPPY by TONI GOFFE

Most men don't even try to make women happy because they know it's a hopeless task. They just don't know what women want. They think they know, but they don't.

They go on with their "Manly ways" of solving their partners problems only to have their efforts rejected, and can't understand why.

It doesn't take long before they give up altogether and may never try again. If only they would ask!
The brave ones that pluck up courage and do ask usually leave it too late and get the answer…
"I shouldn't have to tell you! You should know already,"
which just confuses them even more…and the hope of any discussion of the subject in the future has been sadly dashed!

So it's down to the pub to be consoled by his male companions, who are much easier to please and make happy. Just buy them a pint and you have an instant rapport and a life long friend. Here they feel safe, they can talk about interesting things like football, rugby, cars, tools and tell jokes etc. If only women liked these things too, how easy life would be.

What follows in this book are the efforts of some brave men who have persevered with this quest, they have not been entirely successful, but have make great inroads into this complicated subject. Read these pages carefully, the ideas are right and would work perfectly but the execution of them is disastrous. Study the pictures carefully and see if you can see what has gone wrong. Read the captions again and try and learn by others mistakes.
GOOD LUCK!

BRING HER TEA IN THE MORNING....

TEST HER SENSE OF HUMOUR...
SURPRISE HER WITH FLOWERS...

BUY HER A 'GIRLY MAGAZINE' TO READ.

ARRANGE A SURPRISE PARTY FOR HER....

TAKE HER OUT FOR A DRINK ....

MAKE A 'SPECIAL' DINNER FOR HER...

EXPLAIN GOLF TO THEM.....

DON'T SHOUT AT HER...

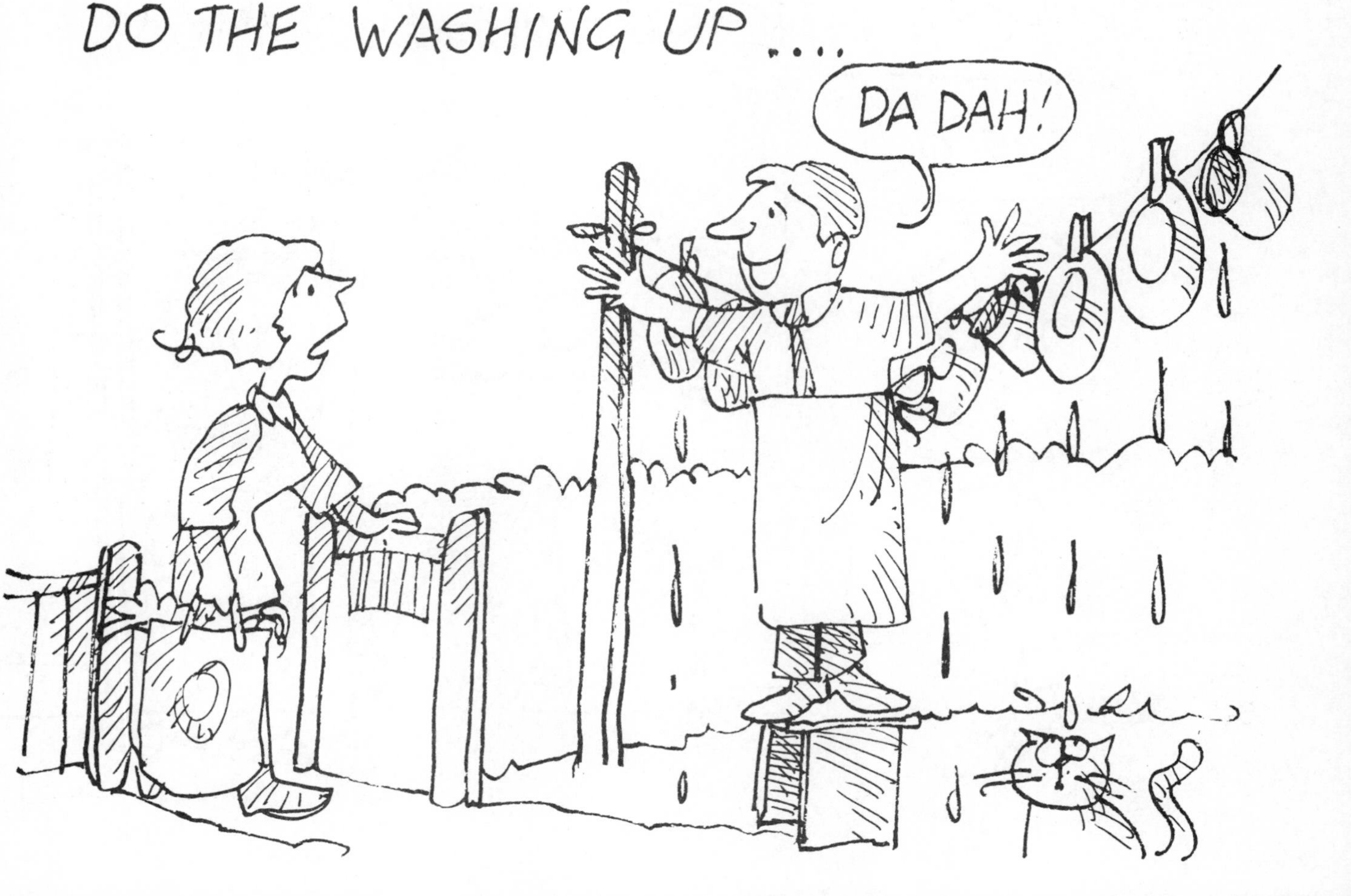
DO THE WASHING UP ....
DA DAH!

DISCUSS TOPICS TOGETHER...

DO LITTLE JOBS ABOUT THE HOUSE...

DON'T KEEP HER AWAKE BY SNORING...

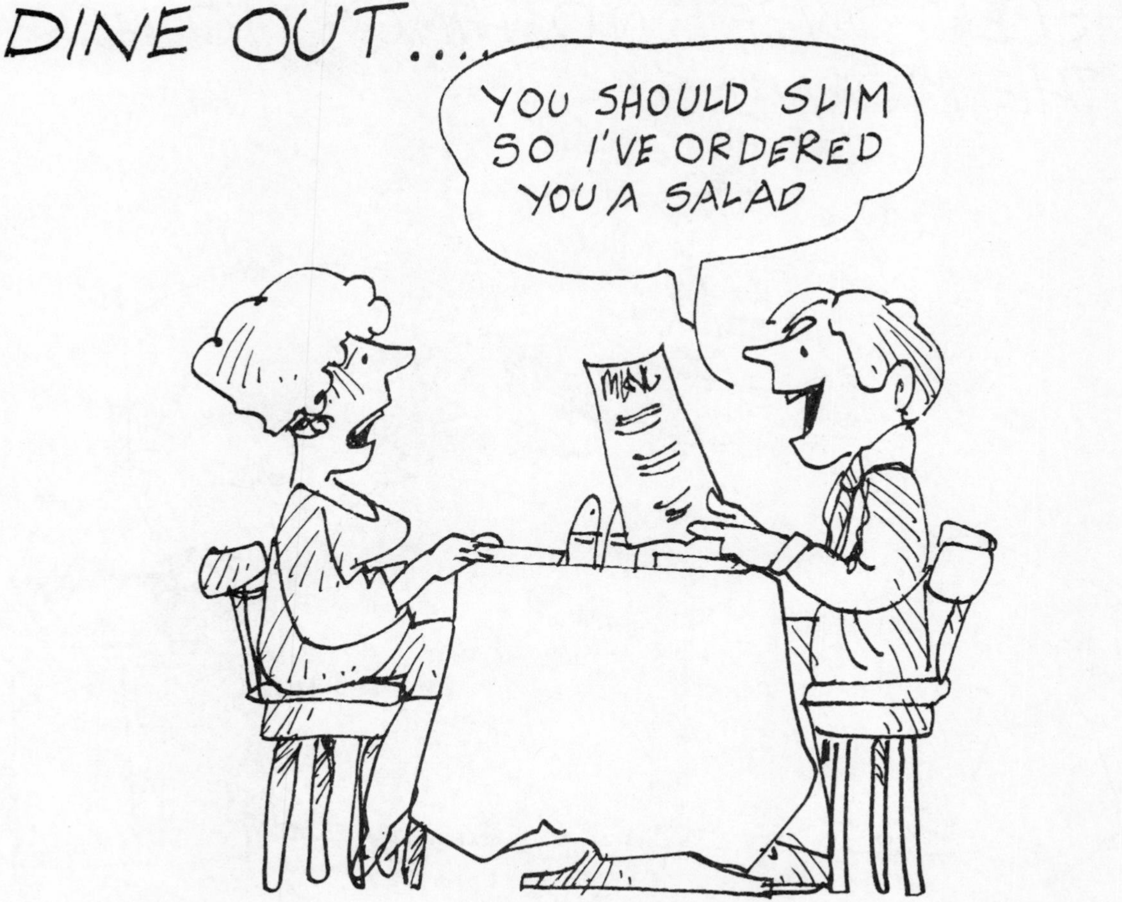
DINE OUT....
YOU SHOULD SLIM SO I'VE ORDERED YOU A SALAD

LOOK AS IF YOU UNDERSTAND
WHAT SHE IS TALKING ABOUT....

SURPRISE HER BY DOING SOME HOUSEWORK ...

BUY HER A PET....

OFFER TO CLEAN OUT HER CAR...

TAKE HER CAR TO THE CAR WASH...

DO SOMETHING NEW AND UNEXPECTED...

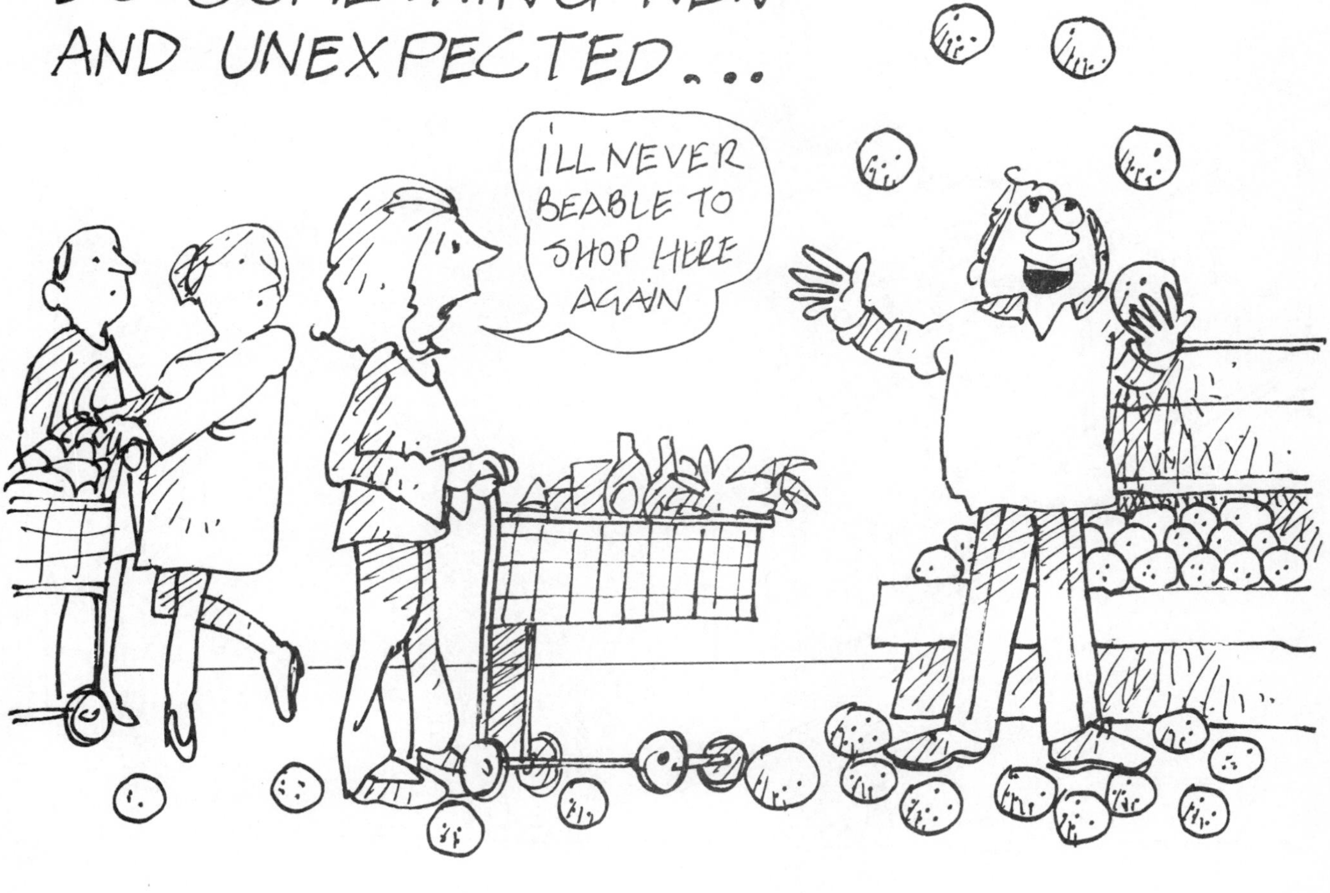

DO 'FUN' THINGS ABOUT THE HOUSE...

SURPRISE HER WITH SOME D·I·Y....

DO SOME GARDENING FOR HER...

SURPRISE HER WITH A FISH POND....

DON'T FORGET HER BIRTHDAY...